THE PORTAGE POETRY SERIES

SERIES TITLES

Bone Country
Linda Nemec Foster

Not Just the Fire
R.B. Simon

Monarch
Heather Bourbeau

The Walk to Cefalù
Lynne Viti

The Found Object Imagines a Life: New and Selected Poems
Mary Catherine Harper

Naming the Ghost
Emily Hockaday

Mourning
Dokubo Melford Goodhead

Messengers of the Gods: New and Selected Poems
Kathryn Gahl

After the 8-Ball
Colleen Alles

Careful Cartography
Devon Bohm

Broken On the Wheel
Barbara Costas-Biggs

Sparks and Disperses
Cathleen Cohen

Holding My Selves Together: New and Selected Poems
Margaret Rozga

Lost and Found Departments
Heather Dubrow

Marginal Notes
Alfonso Brezmes

The Almost-Children
Cassondra Windwalker

Meditations of a Beast
Kristine Ong Muslim

PRAISE FOR

WILDFIRE

Poetry and Theater are the most tasking of the arts. It takes a driven mind to be capable of sustained brilliance. Very few poets writing today have Ms. Rosen's range. In her work, we get both Frank Capra and Orpheus. The micro and the macro.

—ISHMAEL REED
National Book Award Finalist
author of *Why The Black Hole Sings The Blues*

In this imagistic and tender collection, *Wildfire* explores grief through many lenses, offering insight into the possibility of language and the frustration at language's limits. In addition to writing about loss as a personal experience, Rosen broadens the scope to include our collective experiences of grief, including climate change and gun violence. A heartwrenching collection that uplifts the delicate ecosystems we are connected through, *Wildfire* invites us to slow down, look closely, and be transformed.

—SUZI Q. SMITH
author of *Poems for the End of the World*

Corie Rosen's new collection of poems, *Wildfire*, is a book full of portent and wonder, exploring the ineffable in everything from a root canal to a grandmother's instructions on how to boil an egg. Rosen's world is one of meaning and wisdom, all underscored with the important question, How are we to live?—especially in the shadow of ancestral trauma and loss. Full of longing and intricate prose, Rosen's poems delight as much as they intrigue. This is a gorgeous collection.

—ERIKA KROUSE
author of *Save Me, Stranger*

Corie Rosen's *Wildfire* is a phenomenal collection of poems for our troubled, uncertain times, yes, but like the best poetry, it resonates across all time. Rosen boldly looks at the big, hard issues that trouble us, yet at the same time, her poems have a grounded intimacy and urgency. The changing earth trembles beneath us, and life, death, time, memory, history, the cyclical and the philosophical, all come into question. She focuses on the hinged moments between before and after where we are changed irreversibly, and she does so with disarming frankness and a facility for mind-blowing imagery. Clear, direct, incantatory, her wise voices rises above us like a kind of homily, or like a book of prayers to the unfaithful about the unknown. I want to go around quoting lines from this marvelous book, and you will too.

—JIM DANIELS
author of *An Ignorance of Trees* and *The Luck of the Fall*

Rosen's collection brings precise, lucid attention to those fiery forces—the "bright burn of time," the suffering of others—that transmute the stuff and cruelty of life into understanding, history, sometimes even beauty. Her probing, skeptical, and finely worked poems are themselves a kind of hope in a harsh season.

—THEODORE MCCOMBS
author of *Uranians*

WILDFIRE

poems

CORIE ROSEN

CORNERSTONE PRESS
UNIVERSITY OF WISCONSIN-STEVENS POINT

Cornerstone Press, Stevens Point, Wisconsin 54481
Copyright © 2025 Corie Rosen
www.uwsp.edu/cornerstone

Printed in the United States of America.

Library of Congress Control Number: 2025941480
ISBN: 978-1-968148-02-7

Cornerstone Press titles are produced in courses and internships offered by the
Department of English at the University of Wisconsin–Stevens Point.

DIRECTOR & PUBLISHER
Dr. Ross K. Tangedal

EXECUTIVE EDITORS
Jeff Snowbarger, Freesia McKee

EDITORIAL DIRECTOR
Brett Hill

SENIOR EDITORS
Paige Biever, Eva Nielsen, Reilly Crous

PRESS STAFF
Karlie Harpold, Brianna Loving, Aja Wolley, Mydasia Zipperer, Abby Paulsen, Josh
Paulson, Lizzy Vitale, Sophie McPherson, Sam Bjork, Madison Schultz, Autumn
Vine, Allison Lange

To Jeff,
who makes things possible

and to Esmé,
for whom I would remake the world.

ALSO BY CORIE ROSEN:

Words for Things Left Unsaid

CONTENTS

PART I.
ALIGHT: WHAT IS

PART II.

IN ASH: WHAT WAS

PART III.

AN AMERICAN SEASON:
ALL THAT MAY YET BE

PART I.

ALIGHT: WHAT IS

Persephone, Dreaming

I have now been forced to wonder
what it means
        to
watch the place you most love
burning—

destruction that can only mean
a permanent end to things.

Like Orpheus looking back
to see his bride one last
before her hand is peeled from his
and
she is blown back, hair flying
and—
then the orange glare,
the stomach curl,
of a definite end.

What did she whisper
in the moment between
his glance and
their final separation?

Did she only stare,
her gray eyes full of sorrow?

Or did she say:
remember and—
look back and
look back again and
look back again at me
if you dare.

Conflagration

There is nothing you can buy or do
no words to speak to stop it
nothing that, once rebuilt
      will fill the gap—

nothing you can swallow
that will coat your tongue
once again with the sweetness
      of—

      the hillside burned

      the big oak turned to ash

      the family
            unroofed
                  unrooted.

There is nothing
you can ever say or do
that will be a substitute for love.

Devotion

What is left to us, in the end
but the voices of the dead,
words we hadn't thought to speak
and their grave wish—

     to mark something

         say something

             build something—

to leave one last pebble settled neatly on
the headstone of this life.

How easy it would be to give up on all that.
To open your palm a final time and
let go of those books, those songs
those words, those buildings.

How easy to let go of the photograph of
a friend, a girl whom you once loved.

Not so easy, Dear One.

Dear One, look and I will show you—

This:
The color of your skin, this
the slant of your left eyelash, this
the crease that forms when
the light moves across your palm.

This:
the flutter of your lash, eyes closed to feel
the last kiss of a sudden rainstorm, this
your hairline damp, this
your face filled with delight.

To look, to see, to know
not a book, a word, or a building, but
the smooth lines of another body, and
the lither of that voice, singing to you
wayward hymns as you lie in sleep.
This holy thing made from
the *ifs* and *ands*
of everyday living.

That sort of love is nothing more than
a common object—
a small and ordinary thing, and
perhaps it is enough.

Cardinal

You must get busy being born
or you must get busy dying
that's what the songwriters tell us
            and
the songs are never wrong.

I want to be busy with birth,
with all that sticky, urgent newness.

I want to open my mouth and
swallow back clean rain
to notice the way it falls
cold and merciful
against my heart.

To feel clean rain on your face is
to live and not be thankless.

Emotion embarrasses us
            but emotion
like the rain,
            is finally—
all we have.

How can you get busy being born when
so much of this life stands behind you?

Already, I feel the pull of the day when
I will look back and not forward—
a day that will want stillness,
a day that will want
a final taking stock.

That day is hemmed by cardinal seams
        by fissures where
had I turned this way or that way
I would be standing
somewhere else right now.

I would not be stepping in from the rain
would not feel my hair and skin going dry now
would not, standing alone
imagine your hand
its pressure on my shoulder
would not hunger at
the memory of
a heat I used to know.

If I could begin again,
        even if
I had to walk, bareheaded
once more through this rainstorm
maybe I could discover a path to knowing when
a good thing arrives
        and
maybe I would find a way to recognize it.

A way to have understood what you meant when you said
come in, get dry, get warm.

Echo

It was a night for ecstasy—
by which I mean, it was a
night for revelry,
by which I mean that
     for some
it was a night for small, white pills.

We were both nineteen that year—
cheap champagne and
sun up on the Macy's Day Parade.

We were so young and
we stayed up to see the sun break
because we understood that this was
what young people did.

No longer young, M. and I spoke again last August.

     A cup of coffee, he'd said. Just one. I'll be in town.

It was a holiday though, and
the mountains had the White River,
the low hills, blooming with lupins,
those tall flowers all gone
purple at their spines.

     It's okay, he'd said.

     There will be other trips. There will be other weekends.

     Yes, alright, old friend, I'd said. I'll see you the next time.

There was no way to guess then,
how quickly that year's lupins would grow faded, how
the high mountain grasses would fold swift beneath
a blaze and then
a sudden, early snow.

How the relief of nothingness might feel
when compared to
all that
had been promised.

While the world gasped, while
our daughters slept, while
we waited for some new drug
with its promise of a greater safety—

Now, when I draw the blinds at night,
I peer out between the remining houses
            and see there
                along the rooflines
that final slip of starlight
not a view to the sky so much as
a visible gap in time.

Eternity, or close enough
pressing up through
black asphalt shingles.

Perhaps, on the other side of that dark space
there lies an afternoon when
M. and I finally meet for coffee.
Maybe, in the bright burn of time,
I've simply mislaid the moment
            lost it in
the pool of that night
when we were both so young.

Then, we drank our cheap champagne and
I drew a bath just in time to see the sunrise
still waiting for that bright morning when
we would rise and
meet our old selves
once again.

Notice Magic

Some days I suspect
that
our sorrow is here
to teach us.

Look, it says:
the sky, a shell
look—
the whorl of white milk in black coffee.

Look, it says:
notice magic—
let all of this suffering and
all this beauty be.

A Thirst for Light

We have, each of us,
an empty cup
set before us on the table.

Past my window, out on the street,
there is the long gray light, the snow,
winter's indifferent bluster.

It will be the same tomorrow,
though by then it will be
impossible to bear.

Tonight, one last time,
we sit on the porch, still hopeful
            our coats zipped high, our necks
            frail inside of our tall collars.

A new year, a new way, and tomorrow
we'll count backwards
by the moon and midnight,
reset the clocks just as instructed
unsure, even at this late hour
            of how
            or where
            or whether—
            we'll arrive.

First Invocation

It takes time to figure out
how to live, how to be
more than air and soil.

Give me time, I pray, and
give me light.

Give me the warm hours of this day
these words, this hope, this comfort
and then, for a time
let me try and try, and
       when I fail
leave me and let me be.

Root Canal

All I knew how to give you
for the pain was language—
the failed elixir of
"I'm sorry," and
"Hurry home."

For you, it was
the buzz of the hungry drill,
the machine tipped and
sick with lust, with whirring.
The dentist leaning over you,
her body blocking the light.

"It won't hurt a bit," I said,
as though it were I and not the dentist
turning the drill, filling the chamber
breathing in the instrument's cruel steam.

"This too shall pass," you said—
a Russianism, left over from
the years when
your father had used it
and before that
from that other time
          the time when
I still believed
in the innocence of all people.

"This too shall pass," you said,
as though folding all of time around us
as though a phrase could obscure your suffering.

This too shall pass—

words for a time unwound, unbent, unwinding
   words to meant only that
   this ache will one day move
   over, away, and through us.

As though, given enough will
we could swallow America's history whole and
digest lost time's sharp edge.

As though our bodies could
break down the past year's
better memories.

Like an orange we shared years ago
on the front steps of my apartment
our legs bare, our feet tanned,
our faces young in the sun of that summer.

This too shall pass.

You might have said it to me
on the afternoon when
we sat eating that orange
that acid, arch and tangy flesh
still miraculous and impossibly sweet.

You'd known, even then
that I would soon say that
I no longer loved you, and
      you'd known
      even then
that I didn't really mean it
because you understood
      even then
that violence takes many forms.

Free Articles

The Washington Post says: 990, 498, 258, 172.

The Washington Post says: deadly weapon.
        No, sorry. Toy weapon.
        No, sorry. Plastic gun.

The Washington Post says: attack in progress; undetermined other.

The Washington Post says: this month, last, and the next.

        But after that, never again.

The Washington Post says: the cold weather, or a car,
        or else what you don't know, that may kill you.

The Washington Post says: they were all children once.

The Washington Post says: 19, 55, 22, 11.

The Washington Post says: they went in need of nothing.
Or else they went in need of all of it—
mercy or medication, love and bread.

The Washington Post says: they had hopes, once, for their children.
The Washington Post says: they had finally found someone to love.
The Washington Post says: the bodies are mostly, almost, already buried.

The Washington Post says you can put something like that in the ground.

The Washington Post says: we weren't there, you know. We didn't see it.
We didn't hear the popping, didn't see the panic rising
        didn't see the fear become despair as they realized it was true.

We didn't know it was as good as done
        already too late for a Wednesday.

The Washington Post says: in our suffering, we are all one people.

        One people, and all of us entitled to buy guns.

The Washington Post says: no one will be spared.
The Washington Post says: you must not be a raven.

Or else perhaps you are one already, and we have misunderstood.

The Washington Post reports you now,
        high browed harbinger,
        you dark-winged flier.

You, who carry a thin leafed branch,
        flung far like a memory,
        like words we know but cannot think of
                or like a low cloud that flutters
                waving with hope from the distant,
                        untouchable, blue beyond.

To All the Good Young Men and Women
I Will Never Know

Goodbye to you
men and women I'd imagined.

Goodbye to the people who sleep
alongside you in your beds.

Goodbye to the thick Texas heat
       and
to the Carolina summer.
These climates like strangers
       laid fast over
the many roads and churches
those forgotten places hold.

Did you know you'd be leaving when
you lay in your bed
the stars spread like homemade jelly
in clumps
      unseen
           overhead.

Surprising, those stars,
sudden bursts of silver
coming all this way to say hello.

      You, who like my father,
      lay awake all evening
      or who, maybe, like me
      speak to light that's long expired.

The memory of your red wagon in the yard

the smell of rain in puddled footsteps,
that forgotten air fresh on your tongue even now
droplets so bright you can almost taste them.

In memory, everything is stilled
        palmed inside a single moment,
        the blanket's scent and the evening breeze
they make you think maybe you too could
do alchemy with recollections,
        distill the good ones down to starlight
        as though anyone knew how.

Other Wests

And then once again—

      morning.

Slow blur of the sheets, no longer crisp
curled and warmed by our bodies.

Outside, maple leaves are blanching
shifting from red to gold—or no—
that is just the last of the winter light.

Before, the maple leaves were green, green, green.

Now, breath held, we wait
for the goodbye of an ordinary weekday, for
the polluting sunlight, for
the turning that fills the room as
we shift into our other selves
into our other bodies, as
we begin to inhabit
our other, daylight forms.

Only in the night do we seek those other selves
      those Other Wests
      those impossible, imagined histories.

Only then do we allow ourselves to remember
      that
there are so many other ways of
living and dying
of being, and of
waiting to be born.

Declension

The woman who knew suffering said:
                the personal is political.

The woman who knew suffering said:
                there is meaning in every action.

The woman who knew suffering said:
                not to choose is itself a form of choosing.

The woman who knew suffering said:
                then again, what do I know?

        Today, I ask myself—what then, are my actions?

        What are the daily shapes my movements hold?

        A list of things I do:

                Stand barefoot in the kitchen, and
                use the switch to light the fire, and
                listen to Brahms at high volume
                when nobody else is home.

I used to drive great distances to
comfort the ones who thought that
their pain was something special
who were certain that their suffering was
a thing no one else had ever seen.

The year I turned nineteen I went
to synagogue with my lover, beat
my chest alongside strangers

whispered prayers of repentance to
a God I'd tried and failed to know.

Even then, I'd understood that
every one of us was guilty.
The same now, here, as in
all the long years before.

What should I do?
Should I pad barefoot up the highway?
Feel steel nails nick at my heel backs?
Put my money in the market?
Or abandon all I own?

I first learned to swim in an indoor pool in California.
The only large boat I have ever been on is a ferry, though
I once attended a wedding on a small harbor cruise.

Still, I listen to Brahms too loud
light the fire, and
against my will
rise early.

There are actions I could take that might mean something else,
though I'm not sure what or how.

Yesterday, an officer stopped two men
out on the street just for speaking.
Their crime—
        a laugh
        their joy, the spark of an unlit fire.

A calling back, the whispering of
something once bright and fine.

That laughter was
        a tiny gleam of expectation
burned into the darkness
        a lighted truth that they
        understood, but
were not supposed to know.

Lazuli

You can take only so much suffering before
you become a liquid, before
your atoms lighten into
that other form.

Not the taller, leaner shape, but
the rounded, fire-burnt one.

The one that's
blue as lapis stone.

The change allows us to
notice pain in the countenance of
the old man on the corner
allows us to
reach a hand across the empty air,
or to look directly at
the twisted car
at the fire-burnt, ruined town.

It leaves our last words,
singed, solidified, and separate
       fallen from our lips into the
       smoke-filled sky, and
       turned, at last, to stone.

Listen

Listen—
you can't ignore it.

Death, like a secret
encoded in the cells of the body,
written in curled letters
            that stand
behind every slanted cloud.

Listen—
to the pulse,
a symphony that rises
to crescendo and then moves
            eventually
toward its ultimate end.

That music is playing now, and
you have no need for answers, and
the questions themselves are
secrets, and
if only you could read them
            you'd see that
they might contain instructions, only
the order is all wrong.

What's left to us now is
to plead time's case and to
hope and hope
and to remember,
the hillside greened—the rain of ash, the
moment just before
the spark that lit destruction.

The purring of the tabby cat,
curled in sunshine
on the stoop.

Now, the rise and fall of
your own chest is
a question that holds tomorrow's answer
as though an answer to all this were
a thing that could be found.

PART II.

IN ASH: WHAT WAS

Office for the Dead

It was the white night of St. Petersburg
that finally made me see
what it means to live in a place
      as separate and as
      northerly as this one.

All day and night
pale light burned across the rooftops
      light on light, light on
      canals, gray light on
      still water.
Light on the brick-sealed bodies
      of
so many men, long dead.

That day, I stood on the canal
shouldered by a crowd of strangers
      and
the cathedral dome shone round and blue
still alive, even at midnight
burning with heat, with sun,
      with destruction
with the lizard heart of this old town.

This place that was once formed
      by need
      and by
urgent, forceful weather.

Those streets, hard pried from marshy Earth
were home to nothing but
the names of those the city had forgotten.

Hands that build the place as they
poured the soil of their own demise.

Back home, the streets I know best are
the pavers of another country
          life there
          the ghost of
another, hot-mouthed, thing.

Next winter, on my street, there will again be
          the orphaned maples
          the snowbound reach of branches
          the mottled fingers of my neighbors
          the blue lip of mountain sky.

But here, where I stand
          in
the Church of the Spilled Blood of the Savior
the stones send a chill up
through my sandaled feet.

All around,
laughter arrives
          untamed and untranslated, and
I am a visitor to this—
a day without end
the dead without names
the heat of this northern summer, and
the voices that sound against the church steps
          so high and so strange
in a language I've chosen not to speak
          in this place that
I might have once called "Home."

Sapsan

What I'd wanted was
to unseal the past, to have
a glimpse of the place before, and of
the place before that—
the one that I believed was still ours
although it lay far from here
      in a country
      you and I had never seen.

What I'd wanted was
      to
touch the edge of the north
      to
toe the salt black of the Baltic
      to
pass through a door and know
a lost place as though
for the first time.

Later, on the Sapsan's seat,
I had wanted the touch of your fingers
but the land slipped back and
startled us
a vaster place than any I had known.

I had thought I wanted
      lukewarm tea
      the plastic package of stale, dry crackers
      flour and salt as tasteless as
      the stories of who we once believed we'd be.

Homecoming is difficult when
there is no home to come back to
when home is a place you can imagine, but
even after you've arrived, is still
one you cannot reach.

Instructions for Boiling an Egg

First, take out the pot
pour the salt
begin to heat the water.

My grandmother used to say
    you must not
    must not
    must not
    watch it rise to foam.

My grandmother used to say
    unless you look,
    water boils quickly, and
    the arc of history is long.

My grandmother used to say
    people can do
    the unimaginable
    the unthinkable.

But look too closely or for too long
    and it will seem
    you've fallen behind.

She used to say,
    slow down
    no point in trying to rush.

Fix enough eggs in a foreign place
    and it begins to feel like home.
    Or else a homecoming.
    Or, later, the only place
    you can remember ever having been.

Know that, because you were born here
that pot with its
white threads of heat and memory
to you, look like
nothing more than
water boiling, rising into steam.

The Red Door

The first time I saw you
        again
        we'd sat
and spoken as if it were days
        not years
            that
            had
            passed.

A white cloth at the table's edge lay
        flat against
the field of a former time.

It was easy to imagine it once—

        red, I'd thought, the only color for our door.
        a red-doored house, filled with
        love's clocks and hours.

        Now,
        in my stilled home,
            no child of mine smiles
                and I wonder what might have been
            (ours, yours).

What do you put in a place hope has abandoned?

False memory of a red door
        and nothing.

How to Say Goodbye in German

These are shells
  these
round cups of
  conch, clam, and oyster.

They hold animal truths,
an ocean's secret histories
  tucked
  deep inside.

We too are squall,
tide-bound, soft-bellied creatures.

We who swallowed
civilization's last treasure
  who tongued
its sole, remaining key.

There is, hidden within my body,
  the morning when
my Great Uncle stood out on the train platform
not as the old man as I would one day know
  but as
a frightened child of five.

He was prepared to say the thing
in his bis nacher
(his good German)

A language in which the words meant both
see you soon, and
I love you forever, and

goodbye,
goodbye,
goodbye.

This morning, he and I pour
syrup on the pancakes
slice bananas, fill the kitchen with
the steam of the fresh waffles.

Our losses are too numerous to count, and
we carry their shells inside us
find cracks where
you can barely fit your fingers,
where the patterns are hidden deep.

Here, in the backyard
on this Sunday
in suburban California.

The grass is too high and
the post of the wooden gate is half-rotted, and
the metal barely latches for
the bougainvillea's pride.

We sit with pancakes on our plates.
The ice sweats in our glasses.

His chair is a lattice of green metal,
paint peeling on both sides.

The leaves of the big palm cast
shadows on our aspects.

Our shells are
        the missing names
        the missing bones
        the half-remembered faces.

What did he think as he sat across from me,
smiling and smoking after breakfast,
the past locked within him
        shells that were known to me
        and buried still
        impossible to find.

Stolen Objects

The photographs
my father brings out
lie flat within the shoebox
liberated from the dusty country
at the closet's back.

As a girl, I was
   small, quiet, scholarly, uncertain.
I did not yet resemble myself as
I would come to be.

The oldest of the photographs are
   black and white
   or sepia colored.

The one he places in my palm is
   an image of my uncle
   young and small and
     set apart
     cloth coated on the stoop.

There are no images of
the ones who turned to ash
the ones who became smoke pillars
the ones who became soap and salt
the ones whose memories live inside a forgotten box
   or a wooden doll
   or a lost pair of shoelaces
the ones whose lives became
stolen objects
   their inheritance, our inheritance
   a thing we have never held.

The Remained

A new year and
        I could have done more, she said
        her round face full of wrinkles.

Since I'd last seen her, it seemed
        she'd aged
a hundred years or more.

She still wears the old black dress
        still
sits just so, cross ankled
still presses her pale lips together
as though she were just about to speak.

Still, she walks the alleys, and
makes a point of touching
the hands of the other mothers.

There were the ones who went missing,
        the ones whose bodies dissolved into ringlets
        the ones whose nameless bones
        curled into a column of blue smoke.

I could have done more, she says
        and
her face is transformed, transfigured
not young
        but
no longer the face of someone old.

Youth lives on inside the wounds of memory.

I wish I understood why
the sunlight seems misplaced around her
       how
it slants back across her shoulders
       how
its bright warmth feels obscene
       how
it looks so much like a hand
tightening around a wrist bone.

I see the way it closes,
       invisible and forceful,
like the deadly line of history
       pressing close at our throats.

My Grandfather Recounts
a Memory of the Future

Daughter of Fortune
American born—
there are things you must know
but never say.

First, the way the salt foam licks
the surface of
the dark sea.

The way the big ships
floated in, finally,
creaking and tired.

The way that, years later,
we waited for work on darkened corners
the way that, even then
      we were
      determined
hands pressed to fists
fingers closed against the cold.

Still, this was better—
      the smell of bread rising slowly
      the water for tea boiling
      time and heat
      working themselves to steam.

New York, Philadelphia, Washington—
places we lived when
nowhere else would take us.

You must understand
    we had no math
    no common language
    no way of accounting for
    what we'd lost, or
    what we stood to gain.

No way to describe
the taste of fish in cream sauce.

No way to sing the songs we'd known
when we were young.

All those knowings and unknowings
    lay
folded within that first moment
when we stood out on the high decks as
water sprayed across the wood beams
    as
our pasts unraveled in the sunlight
    and
we turned to look at out at that glittering view
that long ago light
suspended in a moment of
sun across the sea.

In a Minor Key

Some days, the sadness
can be so loud that it is difficult to hear
        that little key,
        so minor—

the one
tapping out 'listen'
the one
tapping out 'soon'
the one
tapping out 'joy.'

Joy, even here—
joy
even in this graveyard
joy
even in the centers of St. Petersburg and Prague.
joy, even here, today
in Salt Lake and New York.

The Baltic Way

My grandmother used to say
that 'love,' well translated, meant
'to hold,' 'to keep,' 'to conquer,'
that one day we'd all love and
rise together
and on that bright morning
the whole world would join hands.

Then, she said, all palms would be welcome
even those too large or slightly sweaty,
even those laced with breakfast's
blackberry jam.

Then, the human race would form
a single, Baltic smile
seen from above, we'd make a ring
                and
our song would be celestial
the tonal promise of a circle
that endless, curving form.

Then, we'd feel a unity
forecast by physics
                and
we'd sing a melody tuned
to a different time.

It would, she said, be a song
we had all once hummed together,
but which on the way
we had somehow lost
                or else

forgotten how to tune.
Because the notes were complicated, and
because we'd been too angry, and
because no one had
ever thought to write it down.

Those notes could be made known again
just by touching our palms together—
by looking up, hand in hand
and listening to the music of the stars.

Story Within a Story

Here, each spring brings snow and
with its fall, fresh metaphor—
        a Pesach
        or
        a passing over
(for the secular, like you and me).

A high note to mark the fact that
we've survived another winter.

Another check mark left on
the stone cave of this life.

So we tell the old stories
                and
after all these thousand years
try again to
make the general specific
to turn ancient myths into
anecdotes
that can be told
over a takeout lunch.

The Bible is many things, but
it sure isn't subtle.

Death is dark and angel-winged—
or so the old texts say.

At the low table, we recite
the four questions:

why, and why, and why, and why this again tonight?

Asked and answered by children who are
still too young to know
more than what we tell them.

Afterwards, we sit and speak of other things, of
summers nights spent beachside.

But at dessert, we whisper of
frogs that once fell from

a charcoal sky like rain skins,
of plagues visited on the deserving, or
if not the deserving then—
the politically damned.

History can make a villain or
a martyr of
even the unsuspecting.

Strange to think that all this wandering through
all of this retelling
          may be
nothing more than myth,
invented and inverted
peculiar as the idea of a
sky-blackening frog rain.

When the long telling is over
spring arrives
          and
the night becomes a celebration—
noodle kugel and sweet carrots and
the salt of my grandmother's soup broth
made for twenty, or this year,
for twenty-four.

The soup recipe holds within itself
a separate history
truer than any story
a heritage that you can taste
in celery and brine.

Refrigerator Cake Takes Time

If Time is invented by Death—
        (otherwise, why track it?)
then what
        (do you know?)
is Time's gift, looking backward?

The refrigerator cake I made today
took four hours to set up.

Maybe that's time's contribution?
A cake that can be made
oven-heat and sunlight free?

If you wait long enough
the cream will yield,
give up its density to you.

It's the one thing that I count on
this compliant, creamy taste.

That, and maybe all the wandering through the desert—
        though forty years does not seem time enough
        for bread to rise, or
        to forget
all the things we've seen.

Synonyms for Blindness

I remember,
three doors down

      he was:

long legs,
      skinned knees,
            flash of spokes turning on a bicycle
as he rode, confident
      through sheets of afternoon rain.

Gears whirring
legs pumping
rich and sizzling smells of dinner
      floating out from the open windows.

How could I have known, then
what to look for?

My eyesight was already failing,
I saw cottonwood blooms
in every season
white puffs that fizzed
the edge of every line.

Like you,
I recognized
each day's soft-lipped luster,
      but
I could barely divide
the autumn reds from
the white slips of
the trees.

Then, he was:

a flash of red shirt
        wheels whirring
        as
a soft-eyed boy
rode on through the haze.

Years later, when
the black edges curled in
to touch the seams of
things long since blurred
to secrets

        he was:

a soldier
welcomed home—
so much taller, and
who no longer waved to me.

I could not see it then, in
the halo of those shorter weekdays,
the steady dip into darkness and
because I could not see it
I could not imagine
that soft-eyed boy
his fingers gripping the rifle.

I could not see
the recollections of
his losses, of his sorrows,
his suffering, now sewn into his skin.

I wish I had realized then
when I still had a little eyesight

    that he was:

    wheels spinning
    time turning
    round and round and
round again
    years before anyone noticed
what we'd done to him
    before anyone else was forced to see.

She Might Have Said

My son was seven
the year we lived there—
wide streets, houses fronted by
lawns speckled with
metal sprinklers.

The lady who grew roses
along her gate lived just
two doors over—
her clusters of bright petals were
something hopeful,
something we longed to see.

After school, the tall man with sad eyes would
walk the three blocks home
alongside my small son.

A neighbor's gift of service,
though not because of an ask from me.

I watched them come
each afternoon,
my fingers on the curtain
my sight blurred
thumb resting in
the warm folds of brown wool.

How different those two were,
the one large and the one tiny body
the little blue backpack
        bouncing
                bounding
        bunching
as they toggled down the street.

You don't have to walk him home, I'd said.
It's only three blocks, I can see him.

Yes alright, I know, and I'm happy to.

I guess he saw that you were
so much smaller than the other children
that those eyes of yours were so starling
your laugh so knowing
your stride, even for one so small,
so confident and bold.

Then, he was only a tall man who
offered you
shelter in his shadow.

I wish I had asked him what he thought about
our neighbor's roses,
about other sorts of flowers
ones he had seen pushing up through
foreign pavements
the ones whose shapes and scents
he'd never thought to know.

Maybe all he wanted was
a familiar voice, and
        to speak
the names of every color,
to recognize the many words for 'flower'
to hear someone say
        I see you
        I will walk with you
        and you are not alone.

Foreshortened

It is not one day
        but
a string of days,
        the mornings spaced like streetlamps—
        darkness that crawls up along
        either side of autumn's gleams.

We are taught to expect
        the shorter days
        the lighted streets
        the epilogues to the poems of Frank Capra
smiling windows that have not forgotten
even time's deep rings.

Because you must forget what
has come before you if
you are going to learn
how to welcome
this new life, this
new fire, this heat, with ease.

Winslow

A hundred years or more since
the last coal-blackened train stopped here
steam-hungry and sweating
screaming for a cooler sky.

More than fifty years since the Shah arrived
swathed in white, for his first visit
       though
like so many other travelers
he was only passing by.

Not far beyond this road, sandstone lines
       trace the lip of the canyon
rocks that once were nameless
       an ocean long deadened before
it was witnessed by human eyes.

Like the thing that's happened here
there are meanings you can only reach toward
facts you cannot master
as you press both palms to serif type.

Painted desert, painted lands
       history painted over.

Cypress, Honeylocust, Barberry, and
the sprawl of Old Monk's pepper.

These, in this heat and at this height are
the few plants that will survive here.

Tumbleweed, they'd called the girl,
sending her down like dried, stiff branches
        losing her
like a tree abandoned to the canyon's sides.

Sometimes, the space between life and death is
only a matter of altitude, of clime.

In the Circle K, just to my right,
two boys are holding chocolate eggs,
the sugar melting fast in their warm fingers.

Hurry and eat, I want to say,
soon Easter will be here, and anyway
delight and comfort are too rare a thing
        to last for long
            in this fevered and high place.

A History of Music

Maybe, after the Big Bang
we all just sat around and waited
molecules skimming slimy air,
pausing for instructions.

Or maybe there were simian gleams
coded like math inside our bellies
the way that birds are really dinosaurs, and
the memory of their lizard tails
lies curled within their blood.

Either way, it's us and you
him and me—us versus them all over, and
        I am not yours, and
        you are not mine, and
we wear our histories so tightly that
many of us are, even now
struggling to breathe.

A line of skin as old as
the countries our stories came from.

For all these years, we'd said
the Jews were slaves, but
it turns out nobody knows for sure how it happened
        and
        being a modern person,
        I can't recall the ancestral things.

It's a metaphor, I think, that
the Angel of Death moved among us
        passing low-linteled doorways
        anointed in the thick blood of sheep.

Just a metaphor, I tell myself
that a handprint was left behind to show
who among us would be lucky.

The world divided once again into
those who would be passed over, and
those who, in the end, would not.

You and them.

Him and me.

Us versus you
and again that.

I still like to think that there were
sack races among the locusts, that
the amphibians did cartwheels, that
the young frogs sang and danced together
in the mire of the Middle Eastern sun.

A long time has passed since
you and I were hopeful palm-sized lizards.

We have lied and stolen from each other, and
        along the way
        we've both learned how to love.

From the steeple of the small church near my house
the bells sing out like bird calls, they
beckon summer children who come running, who
        like me, cannot recall
        the memory of what once happened, and so
        cannot know that boundless season
        that other thing
        all that might have been.

PART III.

AN AMERICAN SEASON:
ALL THAT MAY YET BE

Saving Days

Is it true that one day may split a life
        into before and after?

In the Julian Calendar, March was
        the first month of a new year—
        a turning,
        a demarcation,
        but one that, today,
        we no longer need.

What do you put into the gap where
something has gone missing?

What comes next, after
Caesar's final scene?

At the Gorgeous Republic's end
who will act as a witness?

Did the Romans know, just before?
Had they begun to worry?
Or did they, like us,
just sit at home, enthralled
watching the whole thing on TV?

We are all guilty of March's bad deeds
        of ignoring the dividing line, that
        sole, deciding moment
        of refusing speech while
        we still could speak.

And so we tell ourselves that
there will be other moments—
times when we might
more safely move toward
the people we might once have been.

January, Again (or What the New Year Brings)

Out in the desert,
farther than the tourists wander,
the land is not as flat as
it may seem.

What appears plate-like is
gently pebbled
arced and laced with cacti, with
chaparral, cassia, and honeysuckle vine.

Here, on this ancient seafloor
a city sits above a memory—
the Earth's primordial ocean
yawning and blue
long before
the first news van was ever seen.

On this last night of December, in
these last hours of the last year's fading,
alongside us, ghosts of
those ancient corals gleam.

Overhead, the moon makes
dancing stars into
groups of sisters, and
a pair of clouds reaches their arms
just past one another
stopping and straining
before giving up
> and sailing on
> into
> the black well of the night.

But you are not from here, and
you do not know about
this kind of evening.

You do not know how to lean back
how not to take the air in greedy swallows
how not to gasp at the sweetness of the desert winter
how not to reach for forbidden things.

We are walking, and now
we've moved too far away from the others
to be safe, we cannot turn our eyes from
the things that creep in the black around us,
from
the flinty stares of the coyotes
who smell the chaos on our skin.

Here, in this night black landscape,
we've come to search out the best of last year—
the last of life's upturned spirits, to
zip the body of our passing age
into its final evening gown.

Tomorrow, the news begins again, and
we'll shelter on the sofa in the daylight
drink our coffee early and,
sound one more tinkling bell in
the low and sad song of our time.

Reckless in the Daylight

You in your Arcadia—
you deduce the patterns of
the leaf shapes
of the
mountain peaks
of the
cries of a newborn child.

You trace the lines
of the
scaled skins of the lizards
who lie
lazy on their warm stones, and
       fall into a deep sleep
       in the blue sunlight.

Like you, the lizard is ready
       to shed himself
       to become new again, as if
such newness were possible
       as though one could
       leave behind
the casing of this former life.

He too is ready
to step away from
what might have been his
had he reached for something better, sooner

if he'd only held his own
hard-won hippocampus in his small and spiny hand.

Finally though,
he abandons himself
reckless in the daylight.

In the same way we used to run from
the last of the long, cold winter hours, the ones
we would look up at through
the thin, long, purple shadows,
when we were still tall and lean and
as full of promise as
all that we'd believed this place could be.

Anno Domini

The root word is *Februarius*
            but
the term itself has a Latin heart—
from the only honest verb
the one that means 'to purify.'

Strange that the month should bear this name
when everyone knows how much
the Romans hated cold.

They called it a white rock—
they called it a monthless season,
they called it a lost art—
a forbidden, hated thing.

In Finnish, the word is "helmikku,"
which means (loosely)
month of the pearl blossoms.

I can imagine Helsinki now,
gleaming and iridescent
capped in weeks of distilled gray
a place that is only ever light or lack of light.
Glister on the buildings like
the raw inside of an oyster,
snow that collects on the bare strips of
low trees' naked boughs.

Here, February is the third month of
a periwinkle winter.
But there are places that I've been
(and these are Time's inversions)
where February is all star-blind heat—
an orison glimmer.

There, Perseus and Taurus lounge southerly, poolside.

Like any pair left alone too long
they smile through long silences at each other
as though theirs were the only mode, the only language.

Theirs the only weather that
anyone had ever thought to name.

Correlates of Immunity

Someday, good luck
        like gold
may show up in your bloodstream—
clear, not as in the mine
but in the mind.

Riches like silver
flowing cool as
the water of the Colorado.

Cold water, enough of it
can be good luck also,
        if you let it—

Like anything that would
(if you make enough space)
protect you,
sustain you,
stand up and
take your hand.

Leap

I don't know why I did it—
there was no sense in looking
      though
I suppose I was curious and
wanted to know what these many strangers
thought my fate might be.

     "You will have a month of highs and lows."

      "You will have a month of regret and stillness."

      "Your history will repeat itself."

      "The worst of history will go dormant,

        seed again, then bloom."

Between the lines
what they all meant was
heart, take heart (or try to).

In a leap year, there is a need
to search for something extra
a prayer or a condolence—
     some way
to reattach this hanger-on
this loose-tooth leftover of time.

On the phone, my mother says:

     "Try not to overthink your own state of being."

She is practical and that's the kind of

clear-cut sounding, meaningless thing
she has always liked to say.

I suppose, for her
Leap Day is a sort of aphorism
neatly packaged and artificial,
like the pink and yellow Easter grass
that will appear on store shelves soon.

                "If you say so," I relent.

                But I'm still unsure of
                how to account for
                this year's imbalance.

Not having to make sense of things
my mother hangs up and
goes back to canning peaches.

On my end, there are the horoscopes
the ones who give predictions of a safer day
I'm still trying to believe.

My father was a leap child
son of the last survivors
magicked into existence
on this extra day
in this pocket of hope and dirty parking lots—
                the hot innards of California.

In the Latin calendar,
the third month is supposed to
bring in a new promise
                one last breath of patience
                before Mars's rage invades.
In America, leap day heralds
the official months of Youth Art and Celery.

For Catholics, it brings on the Pascal Moon and
the holy rites of Easter, though
if you'd lived in the U.S. in the fifties
you would have known Leap Day as the final hours of
the National Month of Frozen Food.

Magpie

The shadow of a bird
against the screen
        and
my daughter, pointing,
still too young to recall the last of
this winter's losses.

Old enough only to say—
        look
this light, this figure.

Look—
the dazzle of expectation,
this first morning of
the new spring.

After Winter

At the vernal equinox, the day's and night's lengths vary
      though
they still and always move toward
the looser end of time.

I've been told that
there was a first night when
the sun lay down and
dreamt of starlight.

But I still don't know why nature insists on
this fast-moving season—
      so moody and so hungry, looking
      strained around the eyebrows
      as though waiting for something more to come.

In school, we were taught that
      latitude determines day length
      that anatomy is destiny
          or, anyway
      that Freud said a sort of similar thing.

The mystery of the constellations and
the boundaries of the known equations
      these are
woolly, unknowable formulations
that all add up to nothing
      or else
swirl into a perfect, liquid math
the truth, locked inside
those numbers within numbers
held within the darkness
      the boundary of pure forms
      the only thing we may ever know is true.

The Memory of an Orange

There is no perfect death
not like a wedding,
some so much more beautiful than the others
            armfuls of lilies
                        optimistic napkins
            all of it pale and
                        arranged just so.

The firing squad is quick,
so too bombs in the early darkness
not like the bombs that can bury you
still alive, for a while.

The hospital death is colorless,
but the most antiseptic.

Maybe, as you lie flat in your white bed,
you can just recall the sweet tang of an orange
the wind on your face as
the leaves fell lakeside
their yellow cascade dropping, open-palmed
into the last of a long day's light.

A memory can be
too bitter and too beautiful
even in a white bed
to go nameless.

This life—
too bitter and too beautiful
to bear it all alone.

May

It is first a word that grants permission
        then
a month that grants release.

The time when classrooms, like great Russian eggs
spring open, spill, and then
stand alone in their stillness.

A time when, crossing campus on my own
I turn to catch the hand of spring.

What, we wonder, should we do with this
our new, our yearly, freedom?

The iced month's jaws hang loose, and
the pleasure books once dandled
now seem as musty as
the library shelves.

Centuries of ideas,
gone stale and unimportant
when the thing is loyalty
when the thing is safety
        or
when the thing is
the shapes of summer greens.

Why waste our time with
phrases and ideas, when
the sky is clear overhead, and
such a fine, pale aquamarine.

Hurry, says the warm air
hurry, says the sunlight
hurry says the pear tree
with its quivering, white blooms.

Like the pear blossoms
we are only briefly laced in time.

In a week, the white cupped flowers will
fall and spread their spent bodies onto
the bricks of an empty campus.
Their pale cascade will stand in stillness
with nobody left to see.

In each end lies
the curled frond of a new beginning.

If you hold your hand up,
        you can almost catch the heat
        of the next summer coming
        beneath that, the pull of another thing.

Other lives, other books, other ages, other bodies
coming up behind us
straining to know what lay within those long buried books,
and
to hear the voice of another kind of spring.

Before

Then it was July,
so hot out on the street that
stepping outside
made the skin of your forehead tingle.
Made your arms, usually so smooth
begin to prick and bead with sweat.

We went anyway, and
we could not have known
what it meant to be there on that morning
so sticky and so separate, shouting
amassed along the street.

We stood close and sang our songs and
listened for other people's footsteps,
tried to collect the language that would help us to
assemble the facts, piece by piece.

Then, we were still lemon-scented and hopeful
        believing that
someday soon, we'd all join hands and breathe.

The Report on Climate Change in August

It was downtown in deep summer,
at least that's what I remember—
hello and good to see you and
how long has it been?

We stood in the atrium
whose high vined fence
was meant to make you forget
the hot sprawl of the city,
the gray and humid air that hung
just on the other side of all that green.

There was the modern world just over there
rendered all in grayscale.
But we stood in the garden
walled and surrounded
and there were
other people drinking cocktails at low tables.

On the roof, we drank our cheap, chilled wine
held the sweaty sides of our thin glasses—
the coldest and least expensive drink
we could withstand in the heat.

You said, leave it alone,
you said, it's only the news, the paper,
you said, run toward this and eventually
it will drive you insane.

You said, you'll fall in
if you stare for too long at this creature,
if not a pool then
a Medusa that will fix you in stone.
You said, what about joy?
You said, what about the everyday things?

You said, it's just a question of place.
This city, this heat, this changed people.
You said, let's run away.
A ranch in cold, snow dense Wyoming.

I said, they don't take our kind, up there.

You said, people like you, you mean.

The phrase buzzed between and expanded,
grew to fill all of the gray heat.

I laughed the way that people do
when you've said something that's surprised them
and I smiled
the way a person smiles when
the world they once loved is lost
because somebody they'd once loved
has accidentally told them something true.

Delicious

We believe we own these bodies
composed of bits of childhood
memories, histories
       lodged between
the shoulder and the heart.

Like the stretch of beach in Ensenada where
our parents used to take us
the small house with
the big, stone fireplace surround.

Mornings, my father would go diving,
bring up abalone—
shells that glittered in the gray morning
the flesh of the helpless creatures
trembling and salted—
and good enough to eat.

Verse for September

In the backyard
the high, purple grass has
just begun to soften.

Autumn, it says, and
autumn again, and
the old world will come back
      if you let it.

An autumn that will swallow your petunias
leave deep creases on your book flaps
touch your fingers and then
just as suddenly
let go of your hand.

I wish I could ask the grasses about
the depth of my sorrow
wish I could explain to the soil that
the summer light is beautiful
but that fact also makes it obscene.

As though beauty were
still a thing that I could worship
if only it would look back and
nod at me with understanding
or with just a little hope
pretending the best of things could last.

Intermittent Fasting

Now the child, a girl,
is curled into her comma
sleeping on her left side

    dreaming

        asking

            burning

                wondering

    — what it is that she is meant to be.

I haven't eaten in three days.

It's as though the excess of my longing
has lodged itself inside my body.

Stomach, legs, and arms,
these can do with days of hunger
can sustain a month (even)
in starvation
        but
this is not so for a country
not so for a child.

A List of Things Lost in November

There, in the drawer, sits
      the neat pile of photos
      the peach house with the siding where
      you once waited on the porch for me.

There is the single daisy
glinting, wrapped in its plastic sheeting.

There is the blue checked shirt
slightly too big in the shoulders.

Tucked up alongside the other memories,
those folded hours and clocks.

Images that lie next to
the pile of discarded papers
these past things tucked away,
like rot, like trash.

Here is everything that might have been—
      yours
      ours
      everybody's.

Yellowed copies of the New York Times
articles I hadn't meant to read but still did—
these headlines of heat and history
left to spoil in this airless drawer
alongside the evidence of
      my forgotten loves
and all those other
      youthful things.

There are So Many Ways to Be a Mother

There are so many ways to be a mother
even if you stand between
that year of your own birth
and the birth of your first child.

Even if you are forever separated from
that second form of punctuation.

There are so many ways to
water the gardenias
to bake the bread from scratch
to wake before the rest of the house
and get the coffee going.

When I say to my best student
that his work is late and that, after all,
I am not his mother,
I am really offering the safety of a deadline
which is itself a kind of love.

Isn't it that same clarity that
first made you a mother?
The clarity of wanting to give this world
to someone else, even if
she didn't share your blood?

When I was eight years old
I asked my mother why
she didn't write it down more.
She said, I suppose it is because
you are my best book.

Then, I knew how perfectly she'd understood me
and for a moment I saw that
comprehension is the whole of love—
the thing that sits within each moment of compassion
because there are so many ways to be a mother
and so many ways to be a child.

In a Season That Does Not Yet Exist

This morning, the memory of summer
rang out—
long and hot, shot like.

In the park near my house
the lilac and lavender
spread their fingers and
threatened to overtake
the edge of the manmade lake.

Next to the water stands the boathouse—
that shabby home for ducklings
built by the ones who believed that
if new and lemon-colored ducks were born
the children would also come.

Far from here, I know a place where
a Spanish sky makes room for steeples
where pilgrims crawl
on the skin of their bloodied kneecaps,
arms raised, lips parted to taste
the drops of
          a final Iberian rain.

Like us, they pray for benevolence
for the abstraction that is goodness
for the once and future cleansing of
their dirty, cobwebbed souls.

In the thick of the summer heat,
maybe they also slip in a prayer for
an ice-cold soda, or

dream of a time when
they'll at last be new and different
when, beaks tucked, wings sprouted,
they'll finally become the flighted creatures that
they'd always wished to be.

A transformation that will see them
looking high up out of doorways
eyes cast to the Eastern skyline
dreaming of a lost season in Santiago
when we might have
raised our eyes to a better shape of nature,
opened our lips to swallow back
that high mountain rain.

Rough Beasts

In January, the desert is
the top of tourist season—
neon lights, rooms on rooms, and
(who knows what sticky thing is
on that bedspread)
hallways so dark and tangled that
I lose myself inside.

     Here, we stand at bright machines.

     Here, we linger at felt-topped tables.

     Here, we call the game a form of hope, instead of
gambling.

Here are people who would not know
and who do not yearn to know
the times or the timing.

Beneath the all-day lights
the hours smooth out and unravel
and it's possible to pretend that
the hour is an invisible shoreline and that
it is only a fair wind
that's pulled our little boats to sea.

On the news: this man lost, that child drowned,
     all of these bad acts
     and still no consequences.
     That young mother missing
     and yet, the whir of the slot machines.

Meanwhile,
        the smoky air.
Meanwhile,
        the girls in their good dresses.

Meanwhile,
        a new year,
        a new beginning
        this new country
        that we have yet to map or even see.

At home, you turn off the TV
sip your tea, and tell yourself
that these things are not your problems
you sing the old song—
that what is happening to other people
is not happening to me.

In the place I once called home,
January is pale light on dark water,
days of sudden warmth and
smog that sits over the city's frame.

In the mountains where I stand now
January brings on a deep cold, like stillness
snow that seeps into our boot heels
and lets us drift.

Who can say if this first day
might mark a time different than
the one that came before it—
who can say what new or old thing
this year may yet turn out to be.

ACKNOWLEDGMENTS

Earlier versions of some of these poems have appeared in the following places:

Konch Magazine

Rattle | The Rattlecast

Cathexis Northwest Press

Big Muddy

Big Muddy's Best of the Year Print Edition

34th Parallel

Airlie Press

Triggerfish Critical Review

Yes, Poetry

No work of art is a singular creation. Many people's efforts went into making this one, especially Dr. Ross K. Tangedal, the Director and Publisher of Cornerstone, who first accepted the manuscript and who has been a delight to work with from the very first. Thanks also to the lovely and talented Karlie Harpold, who provided thoughtful and detailed editorial guidance and whose insights made this a better book. Lizzy Vitale created a bold and dynamic cover. Sam Bjork and Sophie McPherson helped bring attention to this project as it made its way into the world. My local writing community has also been invaluable, especially the faculty and members of the Lighthouse Writers' Workshop, who have offered me a literary refuge in my adopted home. Andrea Dupree, Michael Henry, William Haywood Henderson, Shana Kelly, Erika Krouse, William Henry Lewis, David Rothman, and Suzi Q. Smith have offered enthusiasm and inspiration. Ted McCombs always knows how to explain me to myself. Amanda Rea and Jenny Taylor Whitehorn have provided space and time, along with many laughs and a disturbing amount of popcorn. My many Lighthouse friends and fellow readers are too numerous to list here, but know that you are all counted. Critic and author Jeff Weiss was the first serious reader of my work in my adult life, and I am forever grateful for his encouragement and insight. T.M. McNally, Peter Turchi, Adrienne Celt, Leah Pate, and all of my friends and colleagues from Arizona State University, you are forever folded within my heart.

No list of acknowledgments would be complete without a deep and heartfelt thank you to my writing teacher and mentor, Ishmael Reed, who first made me believe that this sort of thing might be possible. As an artist, his work is legendary, but the time and energy he has spent mentoring me and others like me is equally profound. I have yet to meet a person of such tremendous intellect and talent who is also possessed of such a bold and generous spirit. He somehow manages to be formidable, inspiring, and beloved all at the same time. His support has been both permission to speak and a lamp to light the way forward, and no page of this book is without his influence.

Finally, and perhaps most importantly, I owe an incalculable debt to my husband Jeff and to my daughter Esmé, who put up with me, inspire me, and make possible all of life's best, brightest, and most beautiful things.

CORIE ROSEN is a fiction writer and poet. Her book of poems, *Words for Things Left Unsaid* (2020) was nominated for the National Book Award, and her writing has been nominated for the Pushcart Prize and has been a finalist for the Katherine Anne Porter Prize for fiction. She is a member of the Lighthouse Writers Workshop and reads fiction and poetry for *The North American Review* and *Salamander Magazine*.

www.ingramcontent.com/pod-product-compliance
Lightning Source LLC
Chambersburg PA
CBHW031436120626
46545CB00006B/2429